THE VO-TECH TRACK TO SUCCESS IN LAW, PUBLIC SAFETY, CORRECTIONS, AND SECURITY

Tamra B. Orr

ROSEN
PUBLISHING®

New York

A special thank-you to librarians everywhere who make researching, reading, learning, and discovering so much more fun. A shout-out especially to Lori Smith and Kim Pinion at the Linus A. Sims Memorial Library in Hammond, Louisiana. You guys make books even bigger treasures than they already are.

Published in 2015 by The Rosen Publishing Group, Inc.
29 East 21st Street, New York, NY 10010

Copyright © 2015 by The Rosen Publishing Group, Inc.

First Edition

Library of Congress Cataloging-in-Publication Data

Orr, Tamra B.
The vo-tech track to success in law, public safety, corrections, and security/ Tamra B. Orr.
        pages cm. — (Learning a trade, preparing for a career)
Audience: Grades 7 to 12.
Includes bibliographical references and index.
ISBN 978-1-4777-7736-7 (library bound)
1. Public safety—Vocational guidance—Juvenile literature. 2. Criminal justice, Administration of—Vocational guidance—Juvenile literature. I. Title.
HV675.5.O77 2014
364.023—dc23

                                                                2013051157

Manufactured in the United States of America

CONTENTS

Introduction 4

Chapter One:
Do You Have What It Takes? Becoming One of Today's Guardians, Protectors, and Caretakers 7

Chapter Two:
Preparing Today for Working Tomorrow 15

Chapter Three:
Right in the Action: A Career in Law 24

Chapter Four:
Our Guardians: Other Law Enforcement Career Options 33

Chapter Five:
Fighting Fire and Saving Lives: Careers in Firefighting and Emergency Medical Services 44

Chapter Six:
Overseeing Safety: A Career in Public Safety and Corrections 54

Glossary 68

For More Information 70

For Further Reading 74

Bibliography 76

Index 78

INTRODUCTION

Everybody likes being the good guy. After all, heroes vanquish the villains. They get into wicked battles and defeat evil. They go up against the odds with bravery, skill, and guts. They defend those who need defending.

When we grow up, we often discover that the line between good guys and bad guys is not always terribly clear, but we still like looking out through the eyes of the hero. We turn on the television and see inside courtrooms, watching as each side argues a position. We watch through dash-mounted cameras as police chase criminals down the highway at triple-digit speeds. We are practically running behind the officers when they crash through a front door to capture offenders hiding inside. We listen and ponder as real detectives mull over clues in cold cases, trying to track down guilty parties. Endless television shows and movies let us walk at a safe distance in the shoes of police officers, prison officials, firefighters, and border patrol agents as they do their jobs. Nightly news reports highlight the courageous work of those same professionals who put their lives at risk to help protect the lives of others.

There is no question that being the good guy is exciting. Just imagining it is frequently enough to get adrenaline going. However, for many people, it is more than just excitement or entertainment; it is the inspiration

One of the noblest "good guys" is the firefighter. Firefighters are willing to put their lives on the line every day to save the lives of others, the ultimate heroism.

for a unique career path and life direction. They don't just sit back and watch the good guys anymore—they become one of them.

The country has seen a steadily growing interest in the fields of public service, law and order, justice, and public and national security over the last decade.

Some experts believe this growth is largely a result of the traumatic events of 9/11. They believe that day inspired countless people to honor the memory of those lost by dedicating their lives to reaching out and helping others.

Another strong appeal is that many of these diverse jobs do not require a four-year (or more) college degree, at least when entering the field. Instead, they require specific training or vocational education—or a combination of the two, which means less time spent sitting in the classroom and more time spent working on the job—a distinct advantage for many young people.

What does it take to be one of the heroes who goes to work each day with the goal of helping other people? This book will show you, plus help you get started on a fulfilling career path that makes the world a better—and a safer—place.

Chapter One

DO YOU HAVE WHAT IT TAKES? BECOMING ONE OF TODAY'S GUARDIANS, PROTECTORS, AND CARETAKERS

Picture a police officer, a firefighter, an emergency medical technician, or a border patrol agent: Chances are, it is someone brave, strong, enduring, or compassionate. Each trait is crucial to becoming one of today's guardians, protectors, and caretakers. Do you have what it takes, emotionally *and* physically?

Developing the Mental Skills

Working in the fields of law, corrections, protection, and security isn't easy. These jobs are tough. It is stressful to the body and the mind. If you prefer a desk and lining up numbers, writing summaries, calculating formulas, or studying reports, look elsewhere. Although communication skills are essential for these jobs, they come after the other skills required, including the following:

- Developing patience
- Modeling compassion and empathy, or understanding

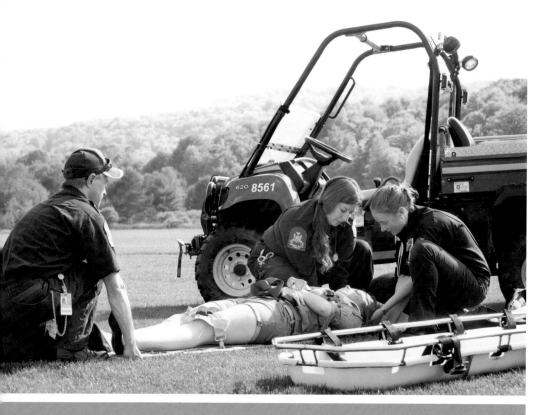

Working with people in pain and in emergency situations often requires a unique blend of personality traits. One must be skilled, efficient, and knowledgeable, as well as calm, compassionate, and kind.

- Demonstrating bravery/courage
- Applying problem-solving abilities
- Expanding multitasking skills
- Working as a team member
- Using good judgment
- Keeping calm under pressure

FIGHTING FRAUD

Daniel Draz had been fascinated by crime for years. "I was always reading mysteries and whodunits as a kid, so it just seemed like criminal justice was a natural fit," he explains. "As a result, I've been in the fraud management business—prevention, detection, and investigation—for years." In the world of business, fraud often occurs when people invest their money in false companies, ideas, and people. Their money is stolen, resulting in billions of dollars in loss annually. "Statistics support that the average company loses about 5 percent of their revenues to fraud," says Draz. "For example, a company with $460 billion in revenues could lose as much as $23 billion annually due to losses from fraud. Globally, this is a big issue."

Draz created Fraud Solutions in 2010. He says fraud occurs in every type of economy, good or bad—but is worst during tough financial times. "The worse things get, the more fraud there is," he explains. "People are trying to get something for nothing or receive financial benefits they were not entitled to." Fraud is not just limited to big businesses either. As Draz says, "Fraud is defined as a 'representation about a material point, which is intentionally or recklessly false and which is believed and acted upon by the victim to his/her damage.'"

While he recommends that students go to college and become certified fraud examiners, he says the skill he looks for most in applicants is being a self-starter. "I want people who are straight shooters—tell it like it is, and can think through problems, and resolve issues using common sense," he says. "Given how much fraud there is," he adds, "there will always be good jobs for those who are interesting in preventing, detecting, or investigating it."

Draz knows his career choice was right. "Being a fraud professional means that I have been involved in some very high-level cases, met some very interesting, unusual, and influential people, traveled to places that most people will never get to, and had experiences that would have never been afforded to me were it not for being in this profession."

Jobs in corrections, security, public protection, and law involve working with people who may be the most challenged that they will ever be in their entire lives. They might be fighting for their freedom in the courtroom or attempting to stay calm following a devastating trauma. Maybe they are sick or injured, or just terribly frightened or worried. These situations require the ability to empathize, yet remain calm and clear-headed. In these jobs, you are the person responsible for getting help. You must be able to think clearly, use good judgment, make sound decisions, and stay steady, even smack in the middle of chaos and confusion.

Everyone responds differently to tense situations. Perhaps someone has had to help a distraught friend. Maybe they have witnessed or been involved in an

The skills you use with an upset or confused friend are similar to abilities you will need to develop for these careers. How do you respond to a friend in need?

accident. They might have seen a fire or had to call 911 to get help when someone was hurt. For others, the closest they've been to any kind of desperate situation has been watching one on television. Some people panic. Others are too frightened to respond. Some remain frozen in place, unable to take action. For these people, getting a job with people who are in dire circumstances might not be the best choice. However, some can stay focused and patient. They make the call, go for help, and take action. They can watch the show and figure out what they would have done in the same situation. They imagine being part of a team, taking, giving, and relaying orders in a streamlined fashion.

Past behavior is a great indication of how you might respond in the future in a career that gets up close and personal with difficult people and events. If you're naturally "cool, calm, and collected," then the addition of experience and proper training may make you one of the best possible guardians, protectors, and caretakers.

CONSIDERING ALL VIEWPOINTS

Amanda decided to pursue courses in criminal justice because they "fascinated the history nerd in me." She believes anyone in the field has to have a passion for following the law. "That doesn't mean you can't have compassion for an individual," she explains, "but if a law is broken, there are consequences." She adds, "Discretion is a helpful trait as well. It's important to realize that people often make mistakes."

Amanda emphasizes the importance of listening to opposing opinions. "Be willing to debate issues and to listen to other people," she says. "Not everyone will feel the same way you do, and you have to be able to talk through issues and take all viewpoints into consideration."

Building the Physical Abilities

Having the right emotional and mental traits for these professions is essential, but the requirements don't stop there. Physical fitness is just as important. People in many of these careers must be able to lift, run, jump, and carry—repeatedly. The requirements often change from one state to the next, but there is one thing they all have in common: they're tough!

For example, the firefighter exam has between eight and eleven tests designed to simulate the main physi-

Putting out fires takes incredibly strong muscles, as well as emotional and mental stamina. It usually requires multiple firefighters to hold a hose with thousands of gallons of water coursing through it.

cal needs found within any firefighting situation. These requirements include wielding a 15-pound (7-kilogram) sledgehammer, carrying a 48-pound (22-kg) hydraulic tool, raising and lowering a heavy ladder, and performing a rescue drag.

Strong muscles are essential, but so is a strong and healthy cardiovascular system. Anyone who has been gaming, watching movies, and sitting at the computer for years and hasn't jumped on a bike, gone jogging, or played sports will likely need to build up muscles and stamina long before attempting any of these intensely

Just like you shouldn't wait until the night before a big test to start studying, don't wait until you're applying for a highly physical job to get physically fit.

physical professions. Consider putting away the junk food and soda, dropping a few pounds if needed, and starting down the path to a healthier, stronger lifestyle now.

Chapter Two

PREPARING TODAY FOR WORKING TOMORROW

D on't wait until after graduation to start exploring career options in corrections, protection, security, and law. Do a little homework, and lay some groundwork now. Start by reading and researching the careers and improving your health. Here are a few ideas to get started:

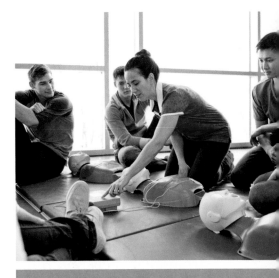

- Get certified in CPR (cardiopulmonary resuscitation) and first aid.
- Join a sports team.
- Become a police cadet to experience involvement in law enforcement.
- Participate in a mock trial.

First aid and CPR are useful skills regardless of what field you go into. Get certified today because you never know what might happen tomorrow.

- Volunteer at crisis centers or emergency shelters.
- Job shadow professionals.
- Apply for any available community internships or apprenticeships (check with a guidance counselor for opportunities).
- Get a part-time job in a related field.
- Find a community mentor to shadow.
- Tour police stations, fire stations, or courthouses.

Larry Long, director of education at Sumner College in Portland, Oregon, agrees the way to prepare for tomorrow is to study hard today. Sumner has a simple motto, "Get in. Get out. Get on with your life" (www.sumnercollege.edu). It offers programs in registered and practical nursing, court reporting, paralegal studies, and being a correctional officer. "We definitely center on career-focused education," says Long. Sumner's correctional officer program lasts for ten months and educates students on working in both the public and private sector. "The job has many perks," continues Long. "It features steady employment, good pay, good health care benefits and retirement packages. Best of all, the landscape of the job changes from day to day, so it is never boring. Being in security gives people the chance to help others."

Sumner's program includes field and patrol operations, juvenile justice, criminology, defensive tactics, transportation and restraints, department of public safety standards, training unarmed security, and spanish. "We do a great deal of role-playing in classes, and all of our instructors are professionals working in

Classes in how to deal with all kinds of medical emergencies help students practice their skills and get accustomed to working with people who are in pain, frightened, or unresponsive.

the field," Long adds. "We help students get employed. Since the wait to get into the public sector can sometimes take a while, students are certified to work in private security as well."

GOING BY THE NUMBERS

How fast a field is growing (or isn't), how much it pays, and how many jobs are available is in constant flux. The most current online *Occupational Outlook Handbook* (www.bls.gov/ooh) provides some great information, but keep in mind it is always changing. Currently, you might find the following:

OCCUPATION	NUMBER OF JOBS (2010)	OUTLOOK
Correctional officer	493,100	5% (slower than average)
Security guard	1,090,600	18% (about as fast as average)
Firefighter	310,400	9% (slower than average)
Paramedic and EMT	226,500	33% (much faster than average)
Police and detective	794,300	7% (slower than average)
Paralegal	256,000	18% (about as fast as average)
Animal control officer	234,900	23% (faster than average)

Exploring Vo-Tech and CTE Programs

Vocational technology (vo-tech) careers and career and technical education (CTE) often share the same goals. President Barack Obama challenged community colleges to help an additional five million students earn their degrees, certificates, and other credentials by the year 2020. In response, the American Association of Community Colleges (AACC) did an in-depth study of how community colleges can achieve this goal. CTE programs are offered in middle schools, high schools, area career and technical centers, community and technical colleges, and other postsecondary universities.

Choosing a Program

Anyone who decides to pursue vocational education has a new set of questions to face. What is the best school? Which program is the most helpful? How will it be paid for? These are important questions.

Begin by researching online. Do these jobs require a certificate or a degree? How many schools or programs are there to choose from? Narrow down the search to those nearby or close enough to travel to. Schedule a visit to the facilities and be prepared with questions. Take along someone you trust, like a parent or mentor, so that they can ask questions, too. Write down everything because after visiting several places, the facts can get mixed up without some notes.

Visiting the campus of a school can give you a feel for the environment. Do you feel like you fit in? Can you imagine taking classes there?

When visiting the facility, listen to the representative, take a tour, and read through the materials the school offers. Then pull out that list of questions and make sure each one is answered before leaving:

1. What kind of tools and equipment does the school provide?
2. Is there any extra fee for the use of these supplies?

3. Who are the instructors?
4. What is the average class size?
5. What percentage of students complete their courses? What percentage are placed in jobs within their fields? How soon? What percentage of students are in debt from student loans at graduation?
6. What is the total cost of the program, including fees for adding/dropping classes, books, equipment, uniforms, or other fees?
7. Is the school accredited? Licensed?
8. Is there any financial or student aid available?
9. What is required for admission?
10. Is the coursework transferable to other schools?
11. What is the amount of crime at the school?
12. What is the total length of the program, and what classes are always included?
13. What is stated in the enrollment contract? (Always read it carefully, as it is a legally binding contract. Never sign it with blanks left open. Keep a copy.)
14. What is the school's refund policy?

Along with listening to the representative—who is paid to make the school look good—also sit in on classes to listen and observe. Are the teachers interesting and classes engaging? Ask students for their opinions. Don't look at one school and stop, if possible. Find competitors and compare. This is your money, time, and potential career, so make decisions carefully.

Paying for the Programs

There's good news and bad news when it comes to financing a vo-tech education. The good news: it costs quite a bit less than a traditional four-year education. After all, there is usually no room and board to cover, and it takes less time to graduate. The bad news: because it costs quite a bit less than a traditional four-year education, it is harder to get scholarships and grants.

Financing vo-tech education starts at the same place as financing any education: by filling out the FAFSA (Free Application for Federal Student Aid, available at http://www.fafsa.ed.gov). Also check out any federally funded programs, as well as your state's department of labor, local labor unions, or sites like Job Corps (http://www.jobcorps.gov/home.aspx). Job Corps is designed for low-income youth between the ages of sixteen and twenty-four. It offers free on-the-job training for eight months to two years in more than one hundred technical areas; free courses at local community and vocational colleges; and even free housing, health care, and career counseling.

Apprenticeships are a wonderful way to learn more about a career and can often lead to financial assistance. In an online interview with Christina Couch for *Bankrate*, Michael Thurmond, commissioner of the Georgia Department of Labor, said, "The benefit there is that (apprenticeship) programs combine vocational training with on-the-job experience. With an apprenticeship, the employer usually pays the student's tuition and gives them a paid job so the student isn't going into debt."

Although funding for vocational careers is sometimes harder to find, it is worth the effort. Start searching early so that you can explore every possible financial option.

Other funding options for vocational education include scholarships, student loans, trade school grants, employment programs, and companies and employers themselves. "The money is out there for trade students, they just have to do their research and apply," Veronica Meury, executive director and vice president of Universal Technical Institute Foundation, told *Bankrate*. "Most students don't realize that there are scholarships for vocational schools that four-year students aren't eligible for."

Chapter Three

RIGHT IN THE ACTION: A CAREER IN LAW

A quick look at popular television shows, movies, and books proves one thing: people are continually fascinated by this country's justice system. These jobs are often portrayed as high-action and thrilling. Whether watching an action movie about the small-town sheriff noticing a suspicious new visitor in town or SWAT (Special Weapons and Tactics) officers surrounding a building holding the bad guys, most people are picturing themselves right in the story.

A career in law can come in many different shapes and sizes. If you like to be in the thick of the situation, a career as a police officer, highway patrol officer, or sheriff might be a good choice. Each one of these positions requires two years or less of education, at least at the entry level.

Being part of a SWAT team terrifies some people—and intrigues and entices others. If you thrive in high-tension situations, a career in the police force may be in your future.

Becoming an Officer of the Law

Few positions in the world of law and security are as intense as those of the police officer, but the job is not the same as it appears on television. While there are adrenaline-filled moments of shooting, chasing, and other intense action, there are even more moments spent filling out paperwork, reading reports, interviewing witnesses, and taking statements. Nonetheless, this job carries a high risk of injury and even death, as it encounters all types of violence and danger. Bravery truly is one of the biggest requirements!

Doing paperwork is one part of police work that is rarely portrayed in movies and television. Nonetheless, desk time is important, so hone those reading and writing skills.

Law enforcement encompasses many different fields. While some police departments require a two- or even four-year degree in criminal justice and related fields (federal offices all require a college degree), others simply require their applicants to have a high school diploma or general equivalency degree (GED). Check with a local agency to determine its specific requirements.

The process of becoming a police officer or sheriff is not quick. The first step is filling out an application, often online. Applicants are usually on a waiting list for weeks to months. Once called, testing begins. A physical agility test ensures applicants are up to the incredible demands of the job. This exam features an obstacle course, including scaling a 6-foot (2-meter) wall and dragging an artificial 150-pound (68-kg) victim ten or more yards. Most tests also require a certain number of pushups, sit-ups, and running. Strength, endurance, and cardiovascular health will be tested. A medical exam records height, weight, and blood pressure; tests vision and hearing; and analyzes blood and urine.

A background check will be done, which investigates a person's employment history, character references, academic records, criminal history, and credit history. It often includes a fingerprint check and may involve interviews with previous employers, teachers, neighbors, or family members.

Psychological testing is done either through a written exam or by an interview with a psychologist. The exam often has hundreds of questions and usually takes several hours to complete. According to the Discover Policing Organization, "The evaluation is a measure of your emotional makeup, your thinking and learning, and how you handle yourself in very difficult situations. The psychological evaluation is to help the police department hire people who are psychologically suitable for the position of police officer."

Next is the written exam. Sometimes it is a series of multiple-choice questions; sometimes it is an essay. And yes, sometimes it is both. These questions are designed to test reading comprehension, problem-solving and judgment skills, memory, and writing skills. Officers fill out an amazing number of forms and reports, so strong communication skills are essential.

This is followed by an oral exam. The ability to express yourself verbally is extremely important. Sometimes this consists of watching videos and responding to them verbally, while being scored. Other times, officers and other staff will ask you questions about the profession and grade your responses. Some of the most common questions include the following:

- Tell the panel about yourself.
- Why do you want to be a police officer/deputy sheriff?
- What is one of your most important strengths/ greatest weaknesses?
- What do you know about the legal elements/ concepts involved in this position?

Remember that during the oral board, applicants are not only being evaluated on their responses but also their appearance, demeanor (or conduct), and communication skills. Often these exams are followed

The long and demanding process of becoming a police officer tests many things, including your persistence, thoroughness, and level of interest. Do you have what it takes?

by a polygraph or lie detector test, which verifies the information the applicant has provided.

To prepare today for becoming a police officer tomorrow, consider doing the following:

• Participate in ride-alongs if the local police department permits them.
• Investigate becoming a police cadet in the community or joining a program like Police Explorers (http://exploring.learning-forlife.org/services/career-exploring/law-enforcement).
• Read police officer preparation books to see what is required to pass.
• Participate in sports.
• Volunteer to increase community connection and to develop empathy.

Once tests are finished, and an applicant has been accepted as a police recruit, it is off to the police academy. These

CHOOSING THE RIGHT CAREER

For the last four years, Brittany, 28, has been a "beat cop." Her training for the job took almost a year. "I went through a vigorous hiring process," she recalls. The physical fitness test was followed by an in-depth written test with everything from math and spelling skills to memorization and critical thinking. "The hardest part was the oral interview," recalls Brittany. "I sat alone in a room with four people as they fired questions at me and graded my responses." Out of the 300 applicants, 30 made the cut—including Brittany. She waited on the list for eighteen months for the call telling her she made it to the next round. Round two consisted of mental and psychological tests, as well as further background checks.

Finally, Brittany was sworn in and her official training began. Following a forty-hour prebasic class of departmental rules, regulations, and paperwork, trainees were sent to the academy for fourteen weeks. "You learn to wear a uniform, march, fight, deal with the public, and shoot—and work out," she says. It was one of the most difficult experiences of her life.

Next came five weeks of field officer training. The five phases merge the trainee from simply observing to the "shadow phase," in which trainees take all the calls, answer the radio, drive the squad car, and write up all of the reports. Then, they're on their own!

"This profession chose me, I did not choose it," explains Brittany. A police shooting occurred in her hometown when she was young. This was her first introduction to the idea of becoming a police officer. Several positive role models also helped her choose to get a college degree in criminology.

Brittany advises young people, "Know how to write! You have to be able to explain yourself on paper." She also encourages teens to be physically fit. "You don't have to be a marathon runner or be able to scale 10-foot walls, but if you can't at least chase someone for a couple of blocks, or be able to fight back, you aren't ready for this career."

Brittany loves her job, but she knows it is not for everyone. "You will work horrible hours, and holidays, and miss time with your family." She also says it affects her personal life. "You become cynical about people sometimes," she admits. "I have nightmares about calls I have gone on. I don't sit with my back to the door, and I'm always looking for the escape route."

Of course, there are wonderful aspects to the job as well. "When you know you've really helped someone, it's amazing," says Brittany. "Just the one call where you make the difference in someone's world puts a new perspective on life. It is calls like that I thrive on and make me smile at the end of the night. I go home knowing I picked the right career. I am blessed to be doing what I always wanted to do, and I wouldn't feel fulfilled if I was doing anything else."

twelve to thirty weeks of training may include classes in any of the following:

- Constitutional law and civil rights
- Regulations, laws, and restrictions
- Accident and criminal investigations
- Self-defense tactics and use of force
- Firearms
- Communication skills
- Report writing
- Patrol and arrest procedures
- Crisis management
- Traffic enforcement
- Courtroom testimony
- Emergency care (first aid and CPR)

Once academy courses are completed, it's time to graduate and finally become a police officer! After six months or more, officers may be able to move up to detective and specialize in a specific type of crime, such as homicide, robbery, narcotics, or traffic. Some decide to become SWAT team members, which requires additional training in close-quarters defensive tactics and special weapons use. (Depending on the particular unit's goals, classes on counter-sniper tactics, helicopter and armored vehicle insertion, explosives, rope skills, and crowd control may also be offered.) Competition for these positions is often incredibly fierce, so applicants should consider going back to school for an associate's or bachelor's degree to increase their chances of being promoted.

Chapter Four

OUR GUARDIANS: OTHER LAW ENFORCEMENT CAREER OPTIONS

Popular reality shows about animal control officers following up on allegations of pet abuse and books about paralegals discovering a technical error changing the entire court verdict prove that not everyone has to be in the crossfire to make a difference. For those who prefer to act less as a warrior and more as a guard, jobs are available as animal rescue officers, border patrol agents, or fish and game wardens. If filing proper paperwork and gathering materials is your strength, the role of paralegal might be ideal.

Interested in security and safety but want a job that's less dangerous than police officer? Consider becoming a security guard. Security guards work in many different locations, including businesses, casinos, hospitals, retail stores, banks, schools, air/sea/rail terminals, and even nuclear power plants. With the increase in terrorist activity in recent years, job opportunities for security guards have been expanding.

Security guards protect everything from people and property to priceless art or large amounts of money. Good observation skills are as important as the ability to stay alert.

Education for security guards is similar to that of police officers, including written, physical, and psychological testing, plus background checks and drug testing. Some employers prefer to hire guards who have an associate's degree in criminal justice or police science, but others want applicants who have gone to vocational college specifically for security guards. Typical curriculum includes training in the following:

- Protection
- Report writing
- Deterring crises
- First aid

After completing training, you are licensed as a guard. By pursuing an associate's degree, you will likely be trained in additional subjects, including criminal law, security management, information security, civil liberties, and investigative techniques. With this degree, possible jobs might include loss prevention agent, gaming surveillance officer, or armored security team leader.

Investigation: Becoming a Private Eye

Another option in law enforcement is becoming a private investigator (PI). PIs are hired to find facts. Books and movies often portray them as wearing fedoras, standing in the shadows, and getting involved in international intrigue. However, most PIs work in legal, financial, or corporate environments. In law firms, they gather witnesses, interview police officers, serve documents, review evidence, and testify in court. In accounting situations, they analyze accounting books of businesses to make sure they are accurate and honest. In the corporate world, PIs focus on protecting companies against competition, checking employees for illegal drug use, or looking into industrial espionage.

Private investigators earn a license in most states. Training is offered at schools like the Detective Training Institute (www.detectivetraining.com) and takes six months or less. Courses focus on the following:

- Background investigation and research
- Skip tracing and locating missing persons
- Surveillance and surveillance photography
- Legal investigations
- Business crime investigations
- Dealing with danger
- Getting started in the career

Business at the Border

A border patrol agent is part of the law enforcement division of the U.S. Customs and Border Protection agency, under the supervision of the Department of Homeland Security. These agents focus on detecting, apprehending, and deterring terrorists and terrorist weapons, as well as preventing the illegal entry of aliens into the country. Most of their work involves doing surveillance, following leads, watching for aircraft, investigating physical evidence, and watching for smuggling activities. Agents are stationed somewhere along the thousands of Mexican and Canadian borders and in coastal waters in the Florida Peninsula and Puerto Rico.

The testing process for the job is similar to that of becoming a police officer. It includes a drug screening test, physical fitness test, medical exam, a background check, and, frequently, a polygraph. In addition, an entrance exam testing logical reasoning abilities and the ability to speak or learn Spanish is administered.

According to the U.S. Customs and Border Protection site, applicants who cannot already speak Spanish are given an Artificial Language Test (ALT). CPB.gov states, "The ALT is a test that helps us predict your ability to learn Spanish. The test may, at first glance, seem intimidating. It is, in fact, based on the grammar and syntax of neo-Latin languages such as Spanish and French. A good grasp of common structures (how the various parts of speech fit together) combined with a thorough reading of the ALT study guide that you receive when you apply will prepare you for this test."

Applicants also go in front of an oral board. The site describes this experience. "The interview consists of situational questions that do not require technical knowledge. The structured interview assesses a candidate's judgment/decision making, emotional maturity, interpersonal skills, and cooperativeness/sensitivity to the needs of others. These qualities are the key to successful performance as a Border Patrol Agent."

Academy training is done in Artesia, New Mexico, and takes less than two months. Classes include the following:

- Immigration and nationality law
- Criminal law and statutory authority
- Spanish
- Border patrol operations
- Care and use of firearms

- Physical training
- Operation of motor vehicles
- Anti-terrorism
- Communications
- Ethics and conduct
- Report writing
- Introduction to computers
- Fingerprinting
- Constitutional law

Protecting the Animals

Sometimes people are not the only ones who need strength, bravery, and protection. Those who enjoy animals and believe they need protection might consider a career as an animal control officer. Enjoying human interaction is important too. According to the National Animal Control Association (www.nacanet.org), animal control officers have four times as many encounters with the public than police officers do!

Animal control officers are in charge of enforcing state laws and local rules regarding the welfare and control of all creatures, from standard pets to exotic or wild animals. Officers may corral a stray dog suspected of having rabies and then trap an escaped boa constrictor at the zoo. They might take an abused horse into protection and then issue a warning to a family for not licensing their dog.

To become a certified animal control officer, applicants need to complete two programs. Each level takes five days and forty hours to finish. (Two additional levels

As an animal control officer, you may find yourself dealing with all kinds of animals, from domestic cats and dogs to exotic zoo animals—or a very large pig!

are available for further training.) Some of the classes taught include the following:

- Animal diseases
- Animal identification
- Animal injury and first aid
- Capture techniques
- Crises intervention
- Courtroom presentation

- Ethics and professionalism
- Euthanasia
- Rabies and quarantine
- Shelter operations
- Animal cruelty investigations
- Crime scene photography
- Officer safety
- Public speaking
- Stress management

To prepare for a job in animal control, consider volunteering at local zoos, humane shelters, and city pounds, plus owning a pet.

Doing the Legal Paperwork

Protecting people means more than keeping them safe from crime. It also means protecting their rights once a crime has been committed. Much of that responsibility is on the shoulders of attorneys and judges, both positions that require substantial law degrees, but the paralegal also plays a vital role. Paralegals and legal assistants are typically hired after getting a two-year associate's degree, although a certificate can be earned in as little as seven months. Currently, more than one thousand colleges have some type of paralegal training program; a quarter of them are approved by the American Bar Association.

Paralegals and legal assistants deal with almost every aspect of a case—and every piece of paper. They help lawyers prepare for hearings and trials. Depending on the size of the law firm, they may do legal

Paralegals are an essential part of any law office, and working in one can give you the chance to be a part of the country's always evolving justice system.

research, write documents such as contracts and mortgages, organize files, present information to lawyers, or review legal materials. Some legal assistants specialize in corporate cases, while others focus on litigation, immigration, or family.

Core paralegal courses include the following:

- Introduction to the law
- Torts and personal injury
- Contracts

TRAINING PARALEGALS

Barbara has been an attorney for more than two decades. Besides working in estate planning and administration and elder law, she also served for five years as the director of paralegal studies at an Oregon business college. What traits does she think students should have if interested in a paralegal career? "Orientation to detail is the most important," says Barbara. "Legal documents have to be really, really precisely completed. Organizational skills and the ability to work effectively with a team are also essential."

Barbara says there are a variety of school options for students. "You can earn everything from a certificate to a master's degree," she says. She suggests choosing a program approved by the American Bar Association (a list of options is available at http://apps.americanbar.org/legalservices/paralegals/directory/allprograms.html). "Before embarking on legal education of any kind," she advises, "work in a law firm or in the courts so that you can see what people in the field actually do every day. It's not like what you see on television!" She also says that paralegals have many opportunities for moving up. "They can get technical positions in law firms or corporate legal departments," she explains. "They may also become claims adjustors or work for companies that sell various products and services to the legal industry, or for those who enjoy working with technology, electronic discovery is a growing specialty."

- Legal research, writing, and civil litigation
- Professional responsibility and legal ethics

A number of specialty courses can be added to the program:

- Business law and property
- Domestic relations
- Alternative dispute resolution
- Environmental law
- Immigration law
- White-collar crime
- Legal document preparation

Tracey Young, former president of the National Federation of Paralegal Associations, stated to *U.S. News* that legal assistant job seekers should "join a local paralegal association to network and get an inside track on employment opportunities."

Protecting others is a noble calling, but one that takes more than good intentions. It takes training, physical and mental strength, endurance, dedication, and time, even behind the scenes. Which pathway you take depends on your personality and preferences. From border patrol agent to animal control officer to paralegal, choices are numerous and options open.

Chapter Five

FIGHTING FIRE AND SAVING LIVES: CAREERS IN FIREFIGHTING AND EMERGENCY MEDICAL SERVICES

Billowing smoke, roaring flames, scalding heat, collapsing buildings (plus long hours spent waiting and preparing to deal with all of these things) are part of being a firefighter. Firefighting is one of the most dangerous and exciting professions in public protection. Hand in hand with the brave firefighter is the skilled emergency medical technician (EMT). Racing to the scene to provide emergency treatment to those in need, EMTs are often the people who ensure victims become survivors instead of fatalities. Both of these jobs require courage, wise judgment, quick thinking, strong skills, endurance—and training.

Whether going into a warehouse fire in search of missing people or dropping down into forest fires to blast the blazing trees, firefighting is a job that takes skills and bravery.

Firefighters have a second home and family. Most firefighters spend many hours on call at the local station. They sleep, eat, relax, and work there with their teams.

Putting Out Fires

How do you imagine a firefighter? Most people see a burning house and a person with a hose on his or her shoulder and an ax in hand trying to extinguish flames. While this image is accurate, it doesn't begin to show the diversity of environments encountered as a firefighter. Firefighters may work in a city fire station, but they may also work in an airport, a chemical plant, an industrial site, or even a forest. Some live in the station while on call, cleaning and maintaining equipment in-between emergency calls, plus conducting practice

STUDYING TODAY FOR TRAINING TOMORROW

Charles Crowther has spent his life involved with fire science. First, he was with the Philadelphia Fire Department for twenty-five years, and then spent five years with the National Terrorism Preparedness Institute. Today, he is the program chair for the Fire Science and Emergency Management Department at St. Petersburg College in Florida (http://www.sp college.edu). He is responsible for determining curriculum and content, plus scheduling, and overseeing instructors. "The job is fast-paced and very challenging," he states. SPU offers certificate training in emergency administration and management, fire inspector, fire investigator, and fire officer.

"Young people want[ing] a career in the Public Safety arena should be encouraged to work hard at whatever educational program they are currently in," he explains. "The skills they bring to the fire or law enforcement employers need not be focused in those areas, as they will be trained in the skills they need for the area they choose. However, it is important that they develop the study habits, and reading and writing skills, needed to be as successful as possible in their specialized training." Crowther emphasizes that young people should also avoid any legal issues, arrests, or convictions because many fire departments will not hire anyone with a criminal record.

The online fire science program at St. Petersburg College is geared toward students who are already employed and allows them the freedom to take classes when they are not working and without having to reschedule their shifts. "Degrees are not required for fire officers in most jurisdictions," adds Crowther.

drills, doing fire inspections, preparing reports, reviewing fire science educational material, and keeping physically fit.

Firefighting is demanding. In addition to coping with the high risk of flames and smoke, emergencies may also include poisonous and explosive gases and chemicals or other hazardous materials. The equipment is heavy, and the protective equipment is hot and hard to wear. The hours are long—most firefighters work more than fifty hours a week, including holidays, nights, and weekends.

Entry-level applicants rarely need more than a high school diploma, although postsecondary education can increase chances of being hired. Educational choices for firefighters can take many different pathways. New firefighters are trained for several weeks at a department's training center or academy. A combination of classroom instruction and practical training is used, and curriculum usually covers the following:

- Firefighting techniques
- Fire prevention

MAKING A DIFFERENCE

Joseph has been a volunteer firefighter in his city for the past five years. He was trained by his city, and commonly goes on runs with full-time firefighters. "We all have the love for the game," he chuckles.

Joseph was surprised by the job's physical demands. "Just wearing the mask is stressful, let alone dealing with the heat of the fire," he explains. "Staying calm during the heat of the battle when you can't see anything means you have to trust your training to get you out safely. One of the most important skills is the ability to think under pressure.

"It takes a certain kind of person to be a firefighter," he adds. "It takes a committed person that cares for others' safety. Most of the fighters I know were born into the life. Volunteer firehouses are made up of years and years of families, from fathers and sons, to daughters and wives."

Megan is only twenty-seven years old, but she has already worked as a 911 dispatcher for three years, then as a firefighter—and then as a paramedic. "As a dispatcher, I knew I loved the field," she explains, "but I felt like I wanted to do more than just be a call for help. I wanted to assist people hands-on."

To get the education she needed, Megan began working for an ambulance company. The company paid for her initial emergency medical technician classes, and then she found a grant for her paramedic schooling. She earned her certifications at a community college.

Young people interested in this profession need two things, according to Megan: passion and compassion. "This isn't the job if you want to be rich," she says. "It is about caring for everyone—not just the people you clinically 'save.' It is the lives you touch one way or another, the lasting impression you leave on family and friends of loved ones who you've helped. Sometimes medics don't realize how a simple gesture of kindness while on a scene can provide a positive memory during a real nightmare. Just knowing you made a difference is what matters," she adds.

- Hazardous materials control
- Local building codes
- Emergency medical procedures (first aid and CPR)
- Equipment use (axes, chain saws, extinguishers, ladders, etc.)

A growing number of fire departments across the country offer apprenticeship programs lasting as long as four years. Some firefighters also choose to attend training sessions provided by the U.S. National Fire Academy. Here, they learn more about anti-arson techniques, disaster preparedness, hazardous materials control, and public fire safety and education.

A number of colleges across the country provide two-year programs in fire science. An associate's degree in fire protection combines fire technology classes with academic courses to help students get a well-rounded education. In addition to taking classes in chemistry, math, writing, and computer science, students study a number of other subjects:

- Hazardous materials
- Firefighting strategies
- Fire detection and inspection
- Fire codes
- Fire protection law
- Occupational Safety and Health Administration (OSHA) standards
- Fire service administration

Different levels in firefighting can be achieved through additional education. For example, at the Utah Fire and Rescue Academy (www.uvu.edu), the Firefighter I level takes 108 hours of training. An additional forty hours brings the student to the Firefighter II level. Additional courses can lead to certification as a fire service instructor, fire investigator, fire inspector, apparatus driver operator, fire officer, hazardous materials technician, and wild land firefighter.

Learning Emergency Medical Services

If you're interested in firefighting, a strong background in emergency medical services is essential. Almost all fire departments require their firefighters to hold at least an EMT-basic certification because approximately

Helping the injured or ill is one of the most compassionate jobs around. Most firefighters must have medical training because more than half of their calls will be medical emergencies.

65 percent of all fire stations provide emergency medical services to the public. (Surprisingly, a firefighter responds to far more calls for medical emergencies than fires!) An increasing number are also requiring their firefighters to have full paramedic training. Although many departments include EMT training as part of the firefighting curriculum, some do not. In these cases, newbies are given a year to become certified on their own.

The terms "EMT" and "paramedic" are often used interchangeably, but they are not synonymous. An

EMT has been trained in either the basic or intermediate level of emergency services. This traditionally takes about six months and includes learning specific skills:

- Performing CPR
- Bandaging wounds
- Treating burns
- Stabilizing neck and spine fractures and other broken bones

EMT courses tend to run between 120 and 150 hours. After finishing the classes, the EMT certifying exam (NREMT) is given. Once passed, it is time to apply to local EMS agencies.

The most advanced level in EMT is the paramedic. This program often takes up to two years to complete, depending on each state's requirements.

A paramedic course usually runs between 1,200 and 1,800 hours of instruction and often requires completion of college-level courses in biology, math, and English. A paramedic is trained to do much more advanced life-saving processes. When classes are finished, you take the NREMT and apply to local agencies.

Some schools offer EMT and paramedic preparation courses. UCLA's Center for Prehospital Care, for example, offers these courses both online and in person. The course covers basic medical subjects such as anatomy, physiology, and medical terminology, plus provides an immediate introduction to concepts like airway management, patient assessment, medical,

Many people today are alive thanks to the caring and skilled work of EMTs and paramedics at accident scenes. A career in these fields is rewarding—but demanding.

legal and ethical issues, and workforce safety (https://www.cpc.mednet.ucla.edu/course/emt-preparation).

For people who are fit and strong, brave, calm under pressure, work well as part of a team, and are able to make wise but fast judgment calls, a career in firefighting or emergency medical services may be ideal. It isn't easy, it is dangerous, and it requires the ability to put out fires and take care of those injured or hurt—but it is a job that saves lives daily!

Chapter Six

OVERSEEING SAFETY: A CAREER IN PUBLIC SAFETY AND CORRECTIONS

Do you feel unsafe when you get up in the morning? Do you worry about being protected on your way to school or coming home from work? Chances are, you don't. And that's because of the hard work of millions of people throughout the country doing their jobs to keep everyone else safe from natural disasters, crime, traffic accidents—and people's mistakes.

Protecting the public is not the responsibility of any single group or organization in this country. Instead, it takes a huge commitment of time, resources, and people to make sure everyone feels safe. From the neighborhood "beat cop" to the director of Homeland Security, from the prison guard to the school crossing guard, people are working every moment to make sure that the world is a safer place. Is there a job waiting for you in that field?

Calling for Help

As incredibly dedicated, brave, and skilled as police officers, firefighters, EMTs, and other public protection

When people call 911, they know someone will answer and help them: the dispatcher. It is the dispatcher's job to make sure every call gets relayed to the appropriate place and receives the necessary help.

workers are, they all depend on one more essential part of the team to do their jobs: the emergency dispatcher. While some dispatchers deal with almost every possible type of emergency, others are specially trained to deal with fire or police departments. Similar positions are available in many states as communications operators, supervisors, and managers.

Being a dispatcher means being able to multitask constantly. Can you listen to music while you study,

DISPATCHING HELP

Greg has been an emergency dispatcher or telecommunications supervisor in Louisiana for a decade. When he works the morning shift, he arrives in the predawn hours. The morning is full of shift changes, report reviews, equipment checks, and radio tests. All shifts include mandatory workout times in the wellness room. "I will change and either get on the treadmill, the stationary bike or the elliptical, punch the punching bag, or a combination for fifteen to sixty minutes, depending on how I feel," Greg explains.

Although Greg had a college degree, it was in an unrelated field. "We do not have any sort of degree requirement here," he explains. "If you spent the money in college, even if in criminal justice, you wasted your time. I've seen many candidates not get hired for being 'too educated.'" Greg's training was done on-site in telecommunications basics, fire dispatch, first aid, CPR, and communications center supervisor.

Greg hadn't planned to stay in the field but fell in love with it. "The ability to multitask is crucial," he advises. "You want people who care, but they have to be able to draw the line between empathy and sympathy. It's OK to care that the caller gets help. It's not OK to let it ruin your day if the person dies from the incident. You have to accept the things you cannot control." He suggests that interested students be able to memorize signal codes and names easily and know when to apply them, take instruction without question, use basic computer skills, and be comfortable speaking on a radio to countless people.

"The best part of this job is being able to help people in their time of need," he explains. One of his favorite moments on the job was when a small child called to report his dog had been caught in a fence. The family was trying to rescue the pet. "I stayed on the phone with him until police could get there. As we talked, the parents freed the dog and the child started yelling through his tears, 'He's OK!' I jumped up and down yelling, 'He's OK!' to everyone, tears streaming down my face—and I am not a crier."

Greg's advice to young people is clear. "You should know this job isn't easy from a stress stand-point, so healthy stress handling is imperative. If you want to help people but do not want the drama of being on the road, this is a great line of work."

Chelsea has been a 911 telecommunications since she was twenty years old because "it runs in my blood," she says. Her parents, grandparents, and uncles are all involved in law enforcement. "I started out as a part-time employee working on a call-in basis and was promoted two years later," she explains. Describing a typical day of work is almost impossible for her. "You never know what type of calls you are going to get. We take calls for wrecks, disturbances, shootings, and medical emergencies." In Louisiana, where Chelsea works, her department has taken more than one hundred thousand calls in a year. "We don't require anything more than a GED," she says. "We do our own training and always offer different types of classes."

"You need patience for this type of work—some days it will become very thin. You also need good typing skills, speech skills, the ability to multitask, and work at a fast pace," adds Chelsea. "I recommend the job to anyone who can handle the high stress. One minute you can have a wreck with a person ejected and possibly dead—and then you will have a woman giving birth as you talk to her. It is a very wide range of emotion."

plus answer a sister's incessant questions, pay attention to the food cooking on the stove, and toss the ball for the energetic dog? How do you deal with a lot of pressure and instant decisions? Do you stay calm and clear-headed if something unexpected happens? Can you take a few deep breaths and remain focused in an emergency? People who answered "yes" to all of these questions might succeed in a dispatching career.

Dispatching is an intense, fast-paced job that requires someone who thinks quickly, speaks clearly, and communicates accurately. Accurate, fast keyboard skills are a must. In this job, dispatchers do the following:

- Monitor emergency phone calls.
- Prioritize the calls (people often call 911 for situations that are definitely not emergencies).
- Obtain accurate location and situation information from the caller, which may not be easy, because the person on the other end of the phone is

often injured or frightened.
- Operate a combination of computers, phones, radios, and recording equipment.
- Send out the proper emergency vehicles and responders to a situation.
- Relay details to police officers, firefighters, and paramedics.
- Keep complete and accurate records of everything that happens.

The educational requirements to be a dispatcher vary from one state to another. For example, in California, applicants must complete 120 hours of training at a certified academy or at least six months of experience working as an emergency dispatcher at another location. In California, dispatchers are often referred to as communications operators. With additional training and experience, this position is often promoted to communications manager and then communications supervisor. Responsibilities increase, including preparing work schedules, evaluating performances, implementing new policies, designing training programs, and keeping in close contact with all public safety personnel.

While some dispatchers are trained on the job, even more enroll in an emergency services dispatcher certificate program, which commonly takes a year to complete. Some of the courses offered include suicide prevention, customer service care, crisis intervention, and stress management. In California, the basic dispatcher course includes courses on technical issues such as telephone and radio technology and law enforcement communications, plus specific classes on missing persons, domestic violence, and child/elder and dependent adult abuse (http://www.post.ca.gov/public-safety-dispatchers-basic-course.aspx). Another option to explore is the International Academies of Emergency Dispatch (www.emergency-dispatch.org), which offers certification in several levels. They base their program on a combination of content, multimedia presentations, and hands-on training.

Working in Corrections

People make mistakes, use bad judgment, and commit crimes. Their reasons may come from ignorance, stupidity, and loss of emotional control such as anger, fear, and frustration. When that happens,

Occasionally, COs teach classes to inmates, including basic English. Knowing how to speak the language makes it easier for prisoners to report medical problems, request their lawyers, or ask for supplies.

IMPROVING LIVES

Gina Larsen is the manager of marketing and recruitment at GEO Group, Inc., one of the world's leading providers of correctional, detention, and community reentry services (www.geogroup.com). GEO has facilities throughout the United States, as well as the United Kingdom, Australia, and South Africa. Larsen states she is part of a team whose goal is "to improve the lives of the people and the communities it serves."

Larsen's job is varied. One day she might be constructing a plan to recruit doctors in California and the next planning to hire security monitors in Alaska. She gets to blend creativity and statistics to ensure that her departments are both efficient and effective.

"Young people should know the security and corrections field provides a rewarding career," she explains. "You are in the business to help people and promote safety, so at the end of the day, you are making a difference and touching people's lives." She also adds, "A job in this field can be grown into a successful career—the sky is the limit in private corrections." Most employees in the corrections field have a college degree, but an associate's degree is enough to get started. "In some cases, we send unlicensed correctional officers to training at the Academy to get certified, and we even pay for it," says Larsen. "This career is not for everyone," she warns. "It is a calling and you must have the desire to want to change lives and help people. The private correctional field is growing. As more and more governments look to the private sector to run their correctional facilities, companies like GEO are looking for talented employees to meet the demand!"

our society turns to the people in corrections to make sure the rights of both the victims and the accused are protected at all times.

Many jobs in corrections can be acquired with either an associate's degree or vocational training:

- Correctional officer (CO)/detention officer
- Community service officer (CSO)
- Youth correctional officer
- Bailiff

Correction officers (COs), also known as detention officers, usually spend their days working with people who have made mistakes or used bad judgment. Some are waiting to go to trial, such as those found in county jails or youth correctional centers. Others have already been convicted and have been placed in state and federal prisons. (COs in federal prisons are required to have four-year degrees.)

COs make sure everyone follows the rules and regulations. If rules are broken, the COs usually are in charge of discipline. Also, COs maintain security, prevent assaults or escape attempts, escort inmates to and from locations, and keep a close eye on all activities. They supervise work assignments; inspect cells; search inmates for possible weapons, drugs, or other contraband; settle arguments; review incoming mail; monitor inmates' health and well-being; and handle any emergencies that arise. Also, correctional officers must keep detailed logs and records about any incidents. Often they keep in touch with other officers by walkie-talkies or cell phones.

Clearly, being a CO is a demanding job, physically and mentally. Jails and prisons operate 24 hours a day, 7 days a week, and 365 days a year, so schedules can be varied. Training for this job is based on the guidelines established by the American Correctional Association. Certain states have regional training centers and there are a number of vo-tech options to earn certification.

Screening to be a CO consists of fingerprinting, an interview, and a pre-employment test (memory and observation, situational reasoning, reading comprehension/deductive reasoning, verbal reasoning, and math). As with most careers in security, protection, and corrections, candidates cannot have any felonies or misdemeanors in their backgrounds. Typically, training is two hundred hours of curriculum and instruction over five or six weeks. A physical agility test is required and involves doing push-ups, sit-ups, and squats, carrying heavy weights, climbing a ladder, and running a quarter of a mile. Good eyesight and hearing are also required.

The community service officer (CSO) does almost the exact same job as the CO, although this person also helps with the processes of booking prisoners, taking inventory, transporting inmates, maintaining equipment and firearms, writing reports, and documenting prisoner behavior. CSOs are expected to complete a correctional officer core course within a year of being hired.

Youth correctional officers are specifically trained to work with minors who have committed a crime such as using drugs, stealing property, or hurting someone. Although requirements vary between states, a sixteen-week program is typical for becoming a youth officer. After that, many states also offer apprenticeship programs.

Getting Insider Advice

Joe Baumann has spent almost three decades as a corrections officer. In an interview with Career Colleges .com, he outlined the skills and attributes every person interested in a career like this should have. "Human temperament and the ability to communicate" were on the top of his list. "The job requires someone who doesn't get flustered easily or overreact to a difficult situation. A good corrections officer doesn't freak out when something goes wrong," he continued, "and he or she is someone who has the ability to communicate with the inmates at a level they can understand. You have got people in prison that are fourth-grade dropouts all the way to Ph.D.s, and you have to effectively communicate with all of them."

His advice to students? "Be ready to work a lot of long hours. You are going to work fifteen-hour days on holidays, and you are going to be working double shifts on your birthday," he says. "Be aware of the impact that it takes on your family life because it takes a heavy, heavy toll."

Finally, another job available within the corrections field without a four-year degree is that of a bailiff or courtroom assistant. The bailiff's main job is to keep a courtroom safe, checking to make sure there are

Verdicts depend on people telling the truth on the stand. The bailiff has all witnesses swear to "tell the truth, the whole truth, and nothing but the truth."

no weapons, bombs, or other types of threats, often by frisking anyone who comes in or out of the room. In addition, bailiffs announce the judge's arrival and make sure he or she has all necessary documents. Bailiffs swear in witnesses and handle evidence. They also keep a close eye on and remove anyone who is not following the rules, such as being disruptive or talking out of turn. Not all trials are done in a single day. When that happens, it is the responsibility of the bailiff to stay close to the jury, escorting them to their hotels or to restaurants.

Bailiffs are often trained on the job, but some schools offer training courses. Graduates earn a peace officer certificate. They usually combine a basic introduction to criminal justice ideas with classes on court security, police and community relations, and law enforcement patrol.

Corrections is a field that calls on many traits, and it is both important and life changing. It is using your energy, skills, time, and education to protect the lives of others. Instead of watching and reading about the world's heroes, you become one of them.

Glossary

adrenaline A hormone made by the body in response to stress, increasing heart and pulse rate.

agility The ability of a person to move quickly and gracefully.

assault A sudden and violent attack.

bailiff A court officer who keeps order in the court.

cardiovascular The system of heart and blood flow in the human body.

compassion Caring about the feelings of other people.

contraband Materials that a person is not allowed or supposed to have.

corrections The methods society uses to deal with convicted criminals.

credentials The qualification or personal quality of a person's background to indicate their suitability for something.

detention Keeping a person in custody or confinement.

discretion The ability to be careful with what one does or says to someone else.

dispatcher A person who relays important information to those who need to know.

distraught Deeply upset or agitated.

empathize To understand and relate to how someone else is feeling.

espionage The practice of spying or using spies to obtain information.

euthanasia The painless killing of a living being suffering from an incurable condition.

felony A crime of some seriousness, such as murder or burglary.

fraud Deception, trickery, or lying to someone for profit.

hydraulic Operated or moved by water or other liquids.

imperative Extremely important or vital.

inmate A prisoner or person who is held in confinement.

misdemeanor A relatively minor or small crime.

paralegal A person who prepares legal documents.

paramedic A person trained in advanced emergency medical treatment.

polygraph A test done to indicate a person's truthfulness.

quarantine The isolation of people.

physiology Biology dealing with the normal functions of living organisms and their parts.

stamina The ability to sustain prolonged physical or mental strength.

surveillance To keep watch over a person or group of people.

syntax The arrangement of words and phrases to create well-formed sentences.

telecommunications Transmitting information over great distances using telegraphs, telephones, radios, or computers.

For More Information

American Correctional Association (ACA)
206 North Washington Street, Suite 200
Alexandria, VA 22314
(800) ACA-JOIN (222-5646)
Website: http://www.aca.org
The American Correctional Association has information
  on various avenues in correctional training, education, and careers.

APCO International
351 N. Williamson Boulevard
Daytona Beach, FL 32114-1112
Website: http:// www.apcointl.org
As the leader in public safety communications, this organization provides a magazine, as well as news and
  announcements in the field. It also provides featured
  jobs within the field in a state-by-state format.

Association for Career and Technical Education (ACTE)
1410 King Street
Alexandria, VA 22314
(800) 826-9972
Website: https://www.acteonline.org
The Association for Career and Technical Education is
  the nation's largest nonprofit education association
  dedicated to the advancement of education preparing young people for successful careers.

Canadian Universities and Colleges Higher Education
  and Employment in Canada
E-mail: news@canadian-universities.net

Website: http://www.canadian-universities.net
Careers in criminal justice within Canada can be found at
    Canadian-Universities.net, Canada's higher-education
    and career guide. The website includes contacts for
    individual Canadian universities.

International Academies of Emergency Dispatch
110 South Regent Street, Suite 800
Salt Lake City, UT 8411
(801) 359-6916
Website: http:// www.emergencydispatch.org
Various levels of emergency dispatching certification
    are available through the International Academies
    of Emergency Dispatch.

International Association of Fire Fighters (IAFF)
1750 New York Avenue NW
Washington, DC 20006
Website: http:// www.iaff.org
Details about the responsibilities, resources, and train-
    ing for careers in fire science can be found at the
    International Association of Fire Fighters website.

Job Corps
200 Constitutional Avenue NW, Suite N4463
Washington, DC 20210
(202) 693-3000
Website: http://www.jobcorps.gov
The Job Corps is a free education and training program
    to help young people learn a career, as well as find
    and keep a good job.

National Partnership for Careers in Public Safety and
     Security (NPCPSS)
16238RR 620 N Suite F, Box 378
Austin, TX 78717
(703) 470-2974
Website: http://www.ncn-npcpss.com
The National Partnership for Careers in Public Safety
     and Security's mission is to "build and support
     career development programs and systems that
     ensure seamless transition by linking and inte-
     grating secondary and post-secondary education,
     professional certifications, and organizational
     recruitment, employment, training, and retention
     systems."

Office of Vocational and Adult Education (OVAE)
400 Maryland Avenue SW
Washington, DC 20202
Website: http://www2.ed.gov/about/offices/list/ovae
     /index.html
The Office of Vocational and Adult Education adminis-
     ters and coordinates programs related to adult edu-
     cation and literacy, career and technical education,
     and community colleges.

Royal Canadian Mounted Police(RCMP)
73 Leikin Drive
Ottawa, ON K1A 0R2
Canada
(613) 993-7267
Website: http://www.rcmp-grc.gc.ca

The Royal Canadian Mounted Police is the Canadian
national police service and operates as a national,
federal, provincial, and municipal policing body.

U.S. Customs and Border Protection
1300 Pennsylvania Avenue NW
Washington, DC 20229
(877) 227-5511
Website: www.cbp.gov
The U.S. Customs and Border Protection agency gives
detailed information on careers within border control.

Websites

Due to the changing nature of Internet links, Rosen
Publishing has developed an online list of websites
related to the subject of this book. This site is updated
regularly. Please use this link to access the list:

http://www.rosenlinks.com/TRADE/Law

For Further Reading

Barrett, Carla. *Courting Kids: Inside an Experimental Youth Court*. New York, NY: NYU Press, 2012.

Bauchner, Elizabeth. *Computer Investigation (*Solving Crimes with Science: Forensics*)*. Broomall, PA: Mason Crest, 2013.

Berger, Sandra. *The Ultimate Guide to Summer Opportunities for Teens: 200 Programs That Prepare You for College Success*. Austin, TX: Prufrock Press, 2007.

Brezina, Corona. *Careers in the Juvenile Justice System*. New York, NY: Rosen Publishing, 2009.

Brezina, Corona. *Careers in Law Enforcement*. New York, NY: Rosen Publishing, 2009.

Evans, Colin. *Evidence*. New York, NY: Chelsea House, 2010.

Evans, Colin. *Trials and the Courts*. New York, NY: Chelsea House, 2010.

Ferguson. *Animal Care* (Career Opportunities). New York, NY: Ferguson Publishing, 2011.

Ferguson. *Problem Solving* (Career Skills). New York, NY: Ferguson Publishing, 2009.

Ferguson. *Public Safety* (Ferguson's Careers in Focus). New York, NY: Ferguson Publishing, 2007.

Freedman, Jeri. *Careers in Security*. New York, NY: Rosen Publishing, 2013.

Gorrell, Gena. *Catching Fire: The Story of Firefighting*. Toronto, ON, Canada: Tundra Books, 2013.

Greenhaven Press. *Career & Technical Education*. San Diego, CA: Greenhaven Press, 2013.

Hagler, Gina. *Careers as a First Responder*. New York, NY: Rosen Publishing, 2012.

Harmon, Daniel. *Careers in the Corrections System*. New York, NY: Rosen Publishing, 2009.

Harmon, Daniel. *Careers in Internet Security*. New York, NY: Rosen Publishing, 2009.

Morkes, Andrew G. *Nontraditional Careers for Women and Men: More Than 30 Great Jobs for Women and Men with Apprenticeships Through Ph.Ds*. Chicago, IL: College and Career Practice, 2012.

Orr, Tamra B. *Careers in the Court System*. New York, NY: Rosen Publishing, 2009.

Porterfield, Jason. *Frequently Asked Questions About College and Career Training*. New York, NY: Rosen Publishing, 2008.

Prentzas, G. S. *Careers as a Paralegal and Legal Assistant*. New York, NY: Rosen Publishing, 2014.

Riddle, John. *Firefighter* (Careers with Character). Broomall, PA: Mason Crest, 2013.

Watson, Stephanie. *A Career as a Police Officer*. New York, NY: Rosen Publishing, 2010.

Bibliography

Arco. *Peterson's Master the Corrections Officer Exam*. Lawrenceville, NJ: Peterson Publishing. 2010.

Blackwell, Amy Hackney. *Career Launcher: Law Enforcement and Public Safety*. New York, NY: Ferguson Publishing, 2011.

Camenson, Blythe. *Careers for Legal Eagles and Other Law-and-Order Types*. New York, NY: McGraw-Hill Books, 2005.

Career Colleges. "Joe Baumann: 27 Years Behind the Walls as a Corrections Officer." Retrieved October 15, 2013 (http://www.careercolleges.com/legal-studies/corrections/interview-professional.html).

CBP.gov "About Border Patrol." U.S. Customs and Border Protection. Retrieved October 15, 2013 (http://www.cbp.gov/xp/cgov/careers/customs_careers/border_careers/bp_agent/faqs_working_for_the_usbp.xml#AboutBorderPatrol).

Coffman, Brittany. Interview with the author. November 10, 2013.

Crowther, Charles. Interview with the author. November 22, 2013.

Couch, Christina. "How to Pay for Vocational Training." Retrieved October 5, 2013 (http://www.bankrate.com/finance/college-finance/how-to-pay-for-vocational-training-1.aspx).

Discover Policing. "More Information About Psychological Testing." Retrieved October 11, 2013 (http://discoverpolicing.org/what_does_take/?fa=q-n-a#-psych).

Draz, Daniel. Interview with the author. October 7, 2013.

EMS1. "Paramedic vs. EMT: Which Path Is Right for You?" EMS 101 Staff. October 14, 2011. (http://www.ems1.com/airway-management/articles/1166255-Paramedic-vs-EMT-Which-path-is-right-for-you).

Fehl, Pamela. *Green Careers in Law, Government and Public Safety*. New York, NY: Ferguson Publishing, 2010.

Forbes, A. S. *Field Guides to Finding a New Career: Public Safety and Law Enforcement*. New York, NY: Ferguson Publishing, 2010.

Golman, Chelsea. Interview with the author, November 15, 2013.

Hood, Greg, Jr. Interview with the author. November 13, 2013.

Larsen, Gina. Interview with the author. November 21, 2013.

Learning Express. *Becoming a Police Officer*. New York, NY: Learning Express LLC, 2009.

Leavitt, Amanda. Interview with the author. October 7, 2013.

Long, Larry. Interview with the author. November 12, 2013.

Paralegal/Money Careers. "Paralegal Job Overview." Retrieved October 1, 2013 (http://money.usnews.com/careers/best-jobs/paralegal).

Smythe, Barbara. Interview with the author. October 10, 2013.

Stevens, Megan. Interview with the author. November 12, 2013.

White, Joseph. Interview with the author. November 14, 2013.

Index

A

American Association of
    Community Colleges, 19
American Bar Association, 40, 42
American Correctional
    Association, 64
animal control officers, 33,
    38–40, 43
apprenticeships, 16, 22, 49
Artificial Language Test (ALT), 37

B

background checks, 26, 30, 34,
    36–37
Baumann, Joe, 65–66
border patrol agents, 7, 33,
    36–38, 43

C

career and technical education
    (CTE), 19
corrections, careers in,
    insider advice, 65–67
    overview, 4–6
    preparing for, 7–23
    requirements, 60–65
CPR, 15, 32, 49, 52, 56
Crowther, Charles, 46–47

D

Department of Homeland
    Security, 36, 54

Draz, Daniel, 9–10
drug testing, 34, 36

E

emergency medical services,
    careers in,
    overview, 4–6
    preparing for, 7–23
    requirements, 50–53
employment programs, 23

F

Federal Application for Federal
    Student Aid (FAFSA), 22
firefighting, careers in,
    insider advice, 46–47
    Joseph's story, 48
    Megan's story, 48–49
    overview, 4–6
    preparing for, 7–23
    requirements, 45, 47, 49–50
first aid, 15, 32, 35, 39, 49, 56
fish and game wardens, 33

G

general equivalency degree
    (GED), 26, 58
grants, 22, 23, 48

I

internships, 16

J

Job Corps, 22

L

Larsen, Gina, 62–63
law enforcement, careers in,
    Barbara's story, 42
    Brittany's story, 30–31
    other options, 33–43
    overview, 4–6
    preparing for, 7–23
    requirements, 25–29, 32
Long, Larry, 16–17

N

National Animal Control
    Association, 38
National Federation of
    Paralegal Associations, 43

O

Obama, Barack, 19
*Occupational Outlook
    Handbook*, 18
Occupational Safety and Health
    Administration (OSHA), 50

P

paralegals, 33, 40–43
private investigators, 35–36

public safety, careers in,
    Chelsea's story, 57–58
    Greg's story, 56–57
    overview, 4–6
    preparing for, 7–23
    requirements, 54–55,
        58–60

R

ride-alongs, 29

S

scholarships, 22, 23
security guards, 33–35
student loans, 21, 23

T

Thurmond, Michael, 22

U

U.S. Customs and Border
    Protection, 36, 37

V

volunteering, 16, 29, 40, 48
vo-tech programs, 19–23, 34

Y

Young, Tracey, 43

About the Author

Tamra B. Orr is a full-time writer and author living in the Pacific Northwest. She is the author of more than 350 nonfiction books for readers of all ages. Orr graduated from Ball State University in Indiana and has been writing incessantly ever since. Her children have investigated many different careers, through firefighting training, volunteering with area search and rescue, and working as security guards. They still haven't made up their minds, but she knows that books like this one will help them discover their many educational options.

Photo Credits

Cover (security guard) picture5479/Shutterstock.com; cover (background), pp. 1, 3 Viappy/Shutterstock.com; p. 5 steve-coleimages/Vetta/Getty Images; p. 8 Cavan Images/Iconica /Getty Images; p. 11 Stockbyte/Thinkstock; pp. 13, 17, 20, 39, 55 © AP Images; p. 14 BananaStock/Thinkstock; p. 15 Hero Images/Getty Images; p. 23 Steve Debenport/E+/Getty Images; p. 24 Vesnaandjic/E+/Getty Images; p. 25 The Washington Times/ZUMA Press; pp. 28–29 Kevork Djansezian/Getty Images; p. 34 Les and Dave Jacobs/Cultura/Getty Images; p. 41 Comstock/Thinkstock; p. 44 Mark O. Thiessen/National Geographic Image Collection/Getty Images; p. 45 Bloomberg /Getty Images; p. 51 Frederic J. Brown/AFP/Getty Images; p. 53 © Mariela Lombard/ZUMA Press; pp. 60–61 Photo by Jack Kurtz/ZUMA Press. © Copyright 2006 by Jack Kurtz; p. 66 Fuse/Thinkstock; cover and interior elements Rhimage/Shutterstock.com (security camera images), Jirsak/Shutterstock.com (tablet frame), schab/Shutterstock.com (text highlighting), nikifiva/Shutterstock.com (stripe textures), Zfoto/Shutterstock.com (abstract curves); back cover graphics ramcreations /Shutterstock.com, banderlog/Shutterstock.com (badge icon).

Designer: Michael Moy; Editor: Heather Moore Niver; Photo Researcher: Karen Huang